Active Earth

Contents

written by Rachel Walker

Evolving planet

Earth has evolved and changed a lot through the long ages since its beginning. In fact, it is still in a constant state of change today. Deep inside the round globe shape of Earth is a core of magma – boiling liquid rock and metals. The mantle is the next layer, made up of hot rocks and more magma. The crust is its outer layer made of hard cold rocks.

Tectonic plates are the huge rocky sections of Earth's outer crust. When they separate and move they crash into each other, reshaping Earth's surface by creating mountains and valleys, causing volcanic eruptions, ground tremors and earthquakes. Coastlines are changed by tsunamis and cyclones.

On the move

Have you heard the expression 'sunrise or sunset'? Actually, the sun isn't moving across the Earth and rising and setting at all – it is Earth that is always moving. It floats like a ball in space, turning as it is pulled by the Moon's gravity.

 Earth spins on its axis as it moves through space on its orbit of the sun. It takes 365 days, that's 1 year, for Earth to revolve around the sun.

The Moon orbits the
Earth every 27.3 days

Although we can't see it, there is an atmospheric field around Earth that is always moving with the planet, held in place by the forces of gravity.

The atmosphere is a moving source of life for every creature of the planet, as it contains essential gases such as oxygen (O_2) and carbon dioxide (CO_2) that plants and animals need to survive.

The atmosphere is vital to:

- absorb energy from the sun
- recycle water and other chemicals
- work with the electrical and magnetic forces to provide a moderate climate
- filter out harmful radiation from space with its molecules like ozone (O_3).

Invisible atmosphere

Watery planet

Oceans cover more than two-thirds of Earth's surface. The oceans are always on the move, and change as large parts freeze over in the wintertime. As well as the massive forces of the waves and ocean currents, driven by the weather, the Moon's gravity pulls on the oceans and creates the tides. The sea level is constantly changing along the coasts. Twice every day, the tide rises up the shore and then goes back down again.

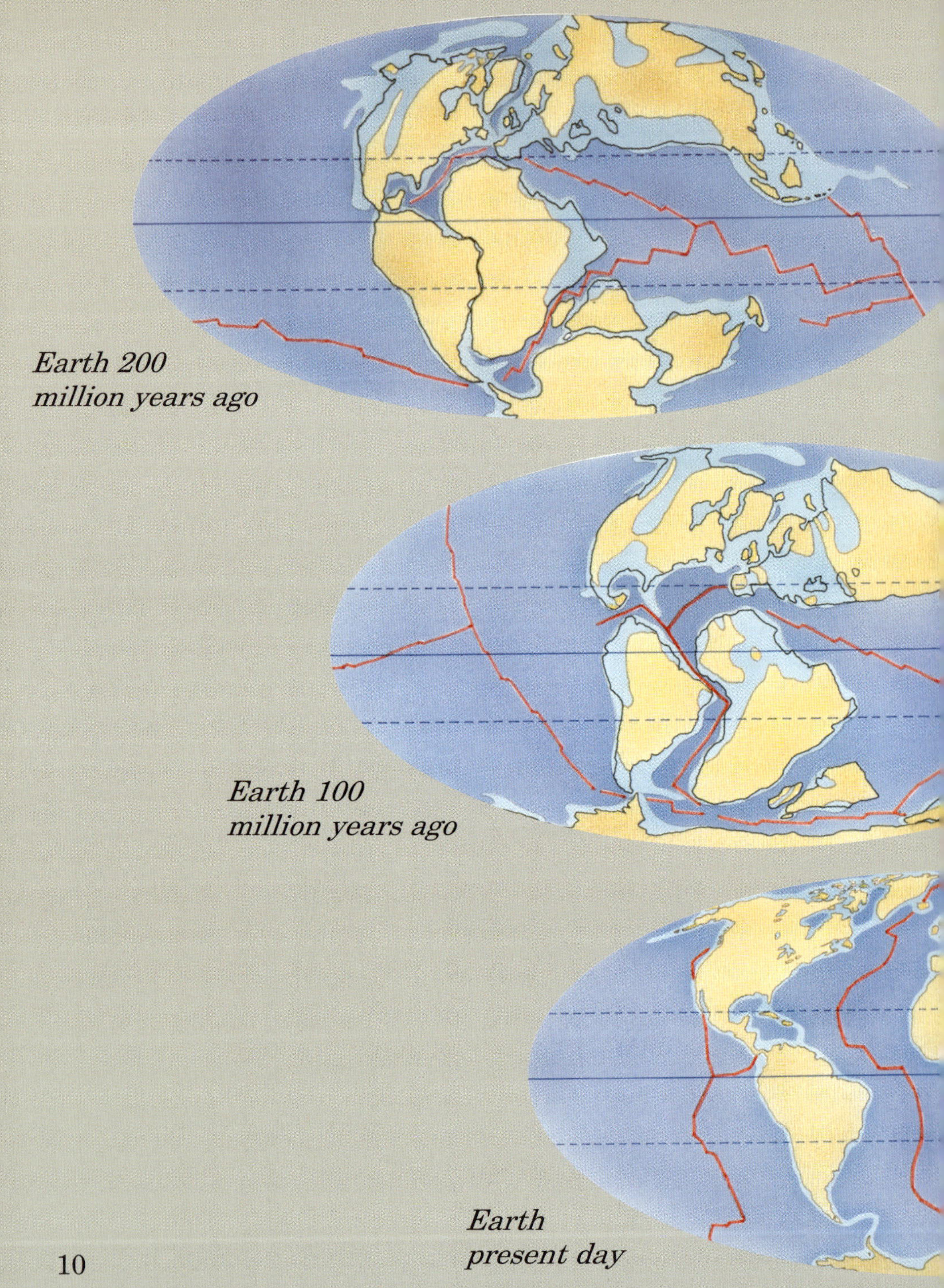

Earth 200
million years ago
Earth 100
million years ago
Earth
present day

Continental drift

Scientists believe that about 250 million years ago a supercontinent existed. This land mass, known as Pangaea, was made up of all the continents on Earth. Over time, these continents have broken apart, and slowly drifted away from one another. This drift continues today, so that the form it takes now is not the final shape of our Earth.

New lands

Islands can form from volcanoes under the ocean. From deep within Earth's mantle, magma rises up and spews lava onto the sea floor. Gradually, this lava builds up, rising above sea level to form new island volcanoes.

Continental islands are bodies of land connected to a continent. They are created by a rise in sea level until only the highest points of the land remain above water. A continental island may be formed when water breaks or cuts through a peninsula, separating it from the mainland.

Coral Islands

Coral islands are formed by coral-building sea organisms known as polyps. Polyps protect their bodies by building limestone walls around themselves. Over many years, these colonies grow large enough to form reefs, which become the basis for new islands. If the sea level drops around an underwater reef, it becomes exposed. Slowly sand and dust pile up on the reef, eventually forming an island.

Go with the flow

Water moves in a cycle,
going around again and
again. Did you know that
the water we use has moved
around the world millions
of times? It comes down
from the clouds as rain, hail
or snow. Most of this water
ends up in the sea. When
the sun shines on the sea, it
turns some of the water into
vapor that rises up in the
air. As the vapor cools, it:

1. changes back to water
2. gathers into clouds
3. falls to earth again as
   rain, hail or snow.

While the water moves
through this endless cycle,
it impacts on the land –
reshaping valleys, moving
river beds and eroding
mountains.

Changing seasons

As Earth spins on its axis all year, it moves closer to the sun, then further away, affecting the amount of sunlight it receives – causing Earth's seasons. In the 365 days that it takes Earth to orbit around the sun, most places will experience four quite distinct seasons. The amount of seasonal difference between regions depends on the sun.

Warming weather

The chances for extreme weather in the future are increasing. We know that warming of the Earth's surface is putting more moisture into the atmosphere, as we can see by the melting of polar ice caps and the rise in sea levels. The ozone layer, which protects us from the sun's harmful UV rays, has become a lot thinner in recent years, and in some places has been completely destroyed!

The Earth's climate
is changing very fast:
something that has not
happened since the end of
the last Ice Age – 10,000
years ago. Scientists
believe that at least
some of the changes are
because of things people
are putting into the
atmosphere: 'greenhouse
gases' (from factories,
vehicles and aircraft),
along with the over-use
of aerosol cans, are partly
to blame. Global warming
is also being made worse
by the cutting down of
forests and the burning of
oil and coal.
People need to take quick
action to protect our
active Earth!